# THE NYC CONSTRUCTION ACCIDENT & INJURY BOOK

***WHAT EVERY WORKER NEEDS TO KNOW AFTER A CONSTRUCTION ACCIDENT***

THE O'CONNOR LAW FIRM
HELPING INJURED NEW YORKERS

**BRIAN J. O'CONNOR, ESQ.**

WORD ASSOCIATION PUBLISHERS
www.wordassociation.com
1.800.827.7903
TARENTUM, PENNSYLVANIA

Printed in the United States of America.

ISBN: 978-1-63385-472-7

*Designed and published by*
Word Association Publishers
205 Fifth Avenue
Tarentum, Pennsylvania 15084

www.wordassociation.com
1.800.827.7903

# THE NYC CONSTRUCTION ACCIDENT & INJURY BOOK

***WHAT EVERY WORKER NEEDS TO KNOW AFTER A CONSTRUCTION ACCIDENT***

**BRIAN J. O'CONNOR, ESQ.**

# TABLE OF CONTENTS

FOREWORD

# WHY I WROTE THIS BOOK

WHILE I FOUNDED THE O'CONNOR LAW FIRM IN 2006 TO fight for injured New Yorkers, I began my career as a defense attorney more than twenty-five years ago. I represented some of the wealthiest property owners, developers and general contractors in the construction industry at one of the largest defense law firms in the country.

I saw first-hand the tactics used by some of the biggest contractors and insurance companies in the business. They will stop at nothing to dispute the facts of your construction accident and cast blame on you for your injuries. After seeing the dirty tricks used by these companies against workers who simply didn't have the right lawyer representing them, I decided that I needed to open my own law firm and make sure I fought for the people that really deserve it – you – the worker.

If you were injured in a construction accident, it can be overwhelming. On top of the physical pain, there may be stress and anxiety in not knowing whether you will return to work, how you will pay your medical bills or how you will support your family. You may also be unsure of whether to contact a lawyer or how to choose the right lawyer for your case.

This book is intended to provide answers to your questions and give you hope and the confidence to know that there is a way forward. This book will provide you with a basic understanding of construction accident law, who may be held responsible for your injuries, how to choose the right lawyer, as well as a blueprint of the legal process.

My hope is that in reading this book, you will be spared some of the stress this uncertainty has caused. I want to empower you with information so that you know what mistakes to avoid and what steps you should take to help your claim. If you decide to speak to a lawyer, this book will provide you with suggestions on what to look for in a qualified construction accident lawyer, questions to ask and answers you can expect to hear.

It is important to understand that you are not alone, that a qualified and experienced construction accident lawyer will take on the burden of the legal process so that you can focus on your recovery. Others have been in your situation before and have come out on the other side ready for life's next challenge.

As an example, I'd like to tell you about Mike, a client of mine that went through a similar experience. Mike was working on the rebuilding of 3 World Trade Center when he sustained serious injuries while falling from a ladder. Mike was concerned that he would not be able to return to work and earn a living to provide for his family. I was able to resolve Mike's case prior to trial for $2.3 million dollars. This was enough money to ensure he and his family would be able to live without worrying about not being able to return to work. I was also able to help Mike obtain social security disability benefits which provided further assistance to him and his family. Of course, you should know that not all cases get the same results and that prior results do not guarantee a similar outcome.

Mike's story is one of many that we have handled at The O'Connor Law Firm.

Once you've looked through this book, you should feel free to call us to discuss your legal issue. My hope is that you will look to us for help when you need it. We are excited to serve you.

## *LEGAL DISCLAIMER:*

This book is an informational consumer guide. It is not legal advice. It is designed to provide helpful information to workers injured in a construction accident in New York City and who would like to know the mistakes to avoid and the steps to take to increase your chances of a successful outcome. I can offer suggestions, explain the legal process, and expose myths. Reading this book does not create an attorney/client relationship. I am not your lawyer until a written retainer agreement is signed for me to be your lawyer. No guarantees can be made as to any result. Each case is different. It is also important to know that each state may have different laws about your type of accident case.

CHAPTER 1

# CONSTRUCTION ACCIDENT FACTS

CONSTRUCTING AND MAINTAINING THE THOUSANDS OF buildings in New York City is not easy. It requires many hardworking men and women— electricians, carpenters, plumbers, pipefitters, equipment operators, ironworkers, masons, laborers and many other tradespeople—engaged in tasks that are often risky and dangerous.

In fact, construction is one of the most dangerous industries in the United States. It is even more dangerous in New York City which employs more construction workers than any other metropolitan area in the country. Federal Bureau of Labor Statistics data show that construction workers make up only 5% of NYC's workforce, but account for 27% of work-related fatalities.

According to the U.S. Bureau of Labor Statistics, there were 5,333 workers who died on the job in 2019. More than 20 percent of private industry fatalities were in construction. The leading causes of construction accident fatalities, previously referred to as "The Fatal Four", are now known as "Construction's Focus Four."

## THE FOCUS FOUR

| | |
|---|---|
| Falls: | 401 out of the 1,102 total deaths in construction (36.4%) |
| Struck by Object: | 170 fatalities (15.4%) |
| Electrocutions: | 79 deaths (7.2%) |
| Caught in-between[1]: | 59 fatalities (5.4%) |

These "focus four" were responsible for almost 65% of the construction worker deaths in 2019. Eliminating the focus four would save more than 700 workers' lives a year in the United States.

### The 10 Most Frequently Cited OSHA Standards Violated

In addition to the dangers of the Focus Four, construction sites across the country still fail to follow safety procedures, resulting in unnecessary and preventable construction worker injuries. According to OSHA, the 10 most frequently violated safety standards in fiscal year 2021 were as follows:

1. Fall protection
2. Respiratory protection
3. Ladders

1 Caught in-between accidents include construction workers killed when caught in or compressed by equipment or objects, and struck, caught or crushed in collapsing structures, equipment or material.

4. Hazard communication standard
5. Scaffolding requirements
6. Fall protection training requirements
7. Control of hazardous energy (lockout/tagout)
8. Eye and face protection
9. Powered industrial trucks
10. Machinery and machine guarding

## NEW YORK CONSTRUCTION ACCIDENT STATISTICS

U.S. Bureau of Labor Statistics further indicate that in New York City, fatal work injuries totaled 59 in 2020, a decline of more than 30 deaths from 2019 (likely reduced, in part, by the covid-19 pandemic). Fatalities in work-related incidents in New York City have ranged from a high of 191 in 1993 to a low of 56 in 2013 and 2016.

In New York City, fatal contact with objects and equipment resulted in 7 deaths, down from 17 in 2019. Falls, slips, and trips accounted for 13 fatalities, a decrease of 11 from the previous year. Worker deaths from exposure to toxic substances or environments totaled 17, unchanged from 2019. Nationally, transportation incidents were the most frequent fatal workplace event accounting for 37 percent of fatal work injuries in 2020.

The construction industry had the highest number of workplace fatalities in New York City with 13, down from 24 in 2019 and 22 in 2018.

Additional statistics:

- Men accounted for 88% of the work-related fatalities in New York City
- Hispanic or Latino workers accounted for 39 % of those who died from a work-related injury in New York City (compared to 23% nationally).
- Workers aged 25 to 54 years old accounted for 64 percent of the city's work-related fatalities in 2020 (compared to 56 % nationally).

## OTHER COMMON CAUSES OF CONSTRUCTION ACCIDENTS

While construction accident fatalities have been in decline in recent years, it is important to make clear that even non-fatal construction accidents can be devastating due to the extreme dangers of working with heavy machinery and extraordinary heights. Some examples of the types of accidents that still occur too frequently:

- Scaffolding and crane collapses
- Falls from ladders, scaffolding or heights
- Injuries caused by falling objects/materials
- Hoist accidents
- Electrocutions and explosions
- Chemical exposure
- Untrained workers
- Excavation accidents

- Demolition accidents
- Heavy machinery accidents
- Forklift accidents
- Power tool malfunctions and missing safeguards
- Slip and falls and trip and falls
- Industrial Code violations
- Shoring accidents

This is just a partial list of the types of accidents that occur on construction sites as each worksite may have different dangers.

## CONSTRUCTION ACCIDENTS CAN CAUSE LIFE THREATENING INJURIES

Even when a construction accident does not result in a fatality, any construction site accident has the potential to cause serious and sometimes catastrophic injuries. Some of these injuries include:

- Head injuries
- Shoulder and knee injuries
- Traumatic brain injury
- Fractured bones
- Spinal cord injuries
- Burn injuries
- Internal organ damage
- Paraplegia and quadriplegia
- Amputations

In an effort to improve the safety of construction workers on jobsites in New York City, new measures were instituted by the City Council that include new requirements that all construction workers obtain 40 hours of safety training. Further, the NYC Department of Buildings has hired additional inspectors to oversee jobsite safety throughout the five boroughs.

While OSHA and local government have improved the safety standards on construction sites over the years, workers' safety is still placed at risk by some owners and contractors who are more concerned with completing a project on time and under-budget than ensuring worker injuries are at a minimum.

It is too often left to you, the construction worker, to watch out for yourself and your co-workers to ensure you are provided with proper and adequate safety devices to perform your jobs. It is my hope that knowing the most common dangers and safety standards violated may provide you with additional awareness while working on your next jobsite.

CHAPTER 2

# NEW YORK LABOR LAW §200, §240(1) AND §241(6)

As mentioned in the previous chapter, the construction industry has some of the highest rates of on-the-job accidents and injuries, which is why there are many special local, state and federal laws in place to protect this particular subset of workers.

In fact, New York State has enacted laws known as Labor Law §200, §240(1) and §241(6) which recognize that the responsibility to provide safe places to work should rest on the people in the best position to do so – the owners and contractors.

## LABOR LAW §200

Labor Law §200 is a statutory version of the common law duty of reasonable care to all workers on a jobsite. Liability under §200 falls into two categories: (1) when a worker sustains injuries as a result of a dangerous condition on a worksite; or (2) when injuries are sustained as a result of the dangerous manner in which the work is performed.

The law requires all worksites to be:

> *"so constructed, equipped, arranged, operated, and conducted as to provide reasonable and adequate protection to the lives, health and safety of all persons employed therein or lawfully frequenting such places. All machinery, equipment and devices in such places shall be so placed, operated, guarded and lighted as to provide reasonable and adequate protection to all such persons."*

Under the "dangerous condition" category, a worker must prove that an owner, contractor or their agent either created the dangerous condition that caused the accident or had actual or constructive notice of the dangerous condition that caused the accident.

When an injury is caused by the dangerous manner or "means and methods" of the performance of the work, the injured worker must prove that the owner, contractor, or their agent exercised supervision and control over the activity that caused the injury and had the authority to stop such unsafe work practices. It is important to understand, however, that the right of a contractor or owner to supervise the work, stop the work if a safety violation is noted, or to ensure compliance with safety regulations and contract specifications is insufficient to impose liability under Labor Law §200 or for common-law negligence. Instead, the evidence must establish that they actually exercised supervision and control over the work performed that caused the injury.

## LABOR LAW §240(1) THE SCAFFOLD LAW

This section, known as the "Scaffold Law," is part of the laws of New York that recognize the unique dangers of working at heights or with equipment and objects that need to be hoisted or secured high in the air. An owner, contractor or their agent will be strictly liable for a worker's injuries if a court determines the statute was violated and the violation was a proximate cause of the accident. [2] This is true even when an owner or contractor is not actively negligent.

Labor Law §240(1) provides that *"all contractors and owners and their agents, except owners of one and two-family dwellings who contract for but do not direct or control the work, in the erection, demolition, repairing, altering, painting, cleaning or pointing of a building or structure shall furnish or erect, or cause to be furnished or erected for the performance of such labor, scaffolding, hoists, stays ladders, slings, hangers, blocks, pulleys, braces, irons, ropes, and other devices which shall be so constructed, placed and operated as to give proper protection to a person so employed."*

Due to the serious danger of construction work and the often-catastrophic injuries that result when either a worker falls from a height or an object falls on a worker or other "gravity-related" injuries, the law recognizes that owners and contractors are in the best position to make sure job sites are safe. Now this does not mean that every fall from a ladder or scaffold results in a

2 A violation of Labor Law §240(1) is considered a "proximate cause" when it is considered a substantial factor in causing the accident. There can be more than one proximate cause of an accident.

Labor Law §240(1) violation. The goal is to make sure workers are safe by forcing owners and contractors to provide safe workplaces, including the appropriate devices and equipment for the tasks workers are required to perform.

As an example of how Labor Law §240(1) is applied, let's look at a worker who falls off a baker scaffold that did not include proper railings across the top platform and also did not have its wheel locks in place at the time it shifted and the worker fell from the top platform. If a court determines that the lack of a top railing was a violation of §240(1) and was a proximate cause of the worker's fall, any evidence that the worker failed to engage the wheel locks on the scaffold and that such a failure may have contributed to the fall will be ignored by the court and the owner or contractor will be 100% liable for the worker's injuries. This is, again, to make sure the owner and general contractor – the people in the best position to ensure a safe workplace – provide the proper equipment.

Once a violation is established and the violation is a proximate cause of the accident, there can be no comparative fault on the part of the injured worker. However, in cases where a worker's own actions are the sole proximate cause of the accident, there can be no violation of the statute. For example, where a worker falls off a ladder because he lost his balance, and there is no evidence that the ladder was defective or inadequate, there is no valid §240(1) claim.[3]

Insurance companies also argue the "recalcitrant worker defense" which may apply in cases where a worker disobeys an

3 See Hugo v. Sarantakos, 108 A.D.3d 744 (2nd Dept. 2013).

order or deliberately refuses to use the proper equipment. The burden is on the owner and contractor to prove this defense.

There have been many cases that appear to be very similar where liability may have been found in one case and not in the other. It is important that you find an attorney who is familiar with the Labor Law statutes as well as the many cases and judicial opinions that have interpreted the statutes in order to ensure you get the best possible outcome for your case. In fact, some of these cases are decided differently depending on the county in which your lawyer files your claim, as the New York State court system is divided into Departments that have jurisdiction over specific counties in New York. For instance, Brooklyn, Queens and Staten Island are under the jurisdiction of the Second Department, while Manhattan and the Bronx are within the jurisdiction of the First Department. A fall from a ladder is often more difficult to win summary judgment via motion in the Second Department than it is in the First Department based upon prior caselaw in each Department.

## LABOR LAW §241(6)

Labor Law §241(6) provides that "*All areas in which construction, excavation or demolition work is being performed shall be so constructed, shored, equipped, guarded, arranged, operated and conducted as to provide reasonable and adequate protection and safety to the persons employed therein or lawfully frequenting such places.*"

While Labor Law §240(1) focuses on gravity related accidents like falls from heights or falling objects, §241(6) is intended to enhance the safety precautions in the context of construction work by requiring compliance with the New York Industrial Code. More specifically, §241(6) imposes a nondelegable duty upon owners, contractors and their agents to provide necessary equipment and comply with safety rules to maintain a safe working environment, provided there is a specific Industrial Code violation causing a worker's injury.

The Industrial Code requires specifications for certain activities being performed and the type of equipment that must be used during the activity, including personal protective equipment such as eye protection.

For example, Industrial Code 23-9.4(e)(1) which provides rules for power operated equipment, directs as follows:

> *"Where power shovels and backhoes are used for material handling such equipment and the use thereof shall be in accordance with the following provisions: Attachment of load: Any load handled by such equipment shall be suspended from the bucket or bucket arm by means of wire rope having* ***a safety factor of four****." (emphasis added).*

If there is a violation of a provision that requires concrete and specific positive commands, such as 23-9.4 (e)(1) cited here, and that violation caused an injury, the owner or contractor will be liable for the injury.

However, not every Industrial Code rule sets forth a concrete and specific command with regards to how a particular task is to be performed. Some Industrial Code rules merely declare general safety standards or restate common-law principles. These more general provisions cannot be used to prove a Labor Law §241(6) violation.

As an example, Industrial Code Rule 23-1.5(c)(2) requires that "all load carrying equipment shall ...**safely support the loads intended to be imposed thereon**." (emphasis added). This rule simply declares a general safety standard without providing a more specific command as to how load carrying equipment should support a load. This type of general rule is not sufficient to support a Labor Law 241(6) claim.

Last, unlike §240(1) where there can be no comparative fault on the worker, under Labor Law §241(6) if a worker was also at fault in causing the accident, any recovery will be reduced by the percentage of the worker's fault.

CHAPTER 3

# WORKERS' COMPENSATION BENEFITS AND THEIR LIMITATIONS

If you are injured in a work-related construction accident in New York, you are entitled to workers' compensation benefits regardless of fault. In fact, in many instances, workers' compensation benefits are a worker's sole remedy against an employer.

## *HOW DOES WORKERS' COMPENSATION APPLY TO CONSTRUCTION ACCIDENT INJURIES?*

Workers' compensation ("WC") is a no-fault benefits program administered through New York State and selected insurance carriers. The New York State Workers' Compensation Board

("WCB") is the state agency that oversees workers' compensation claims. In order to properly file a WC claim, a worker must:

- Report the accident to your employer, in writing, within 30 days
- File an employee claim form (form C-3) with the WC Board within 2 years
- Obtain medical treatment from a WC approved physician, and
- File a doctor's initial report (form C-4) from your treating physician

Because it is a no-fault system, a worker does not need to prove fault in order to start collecting WC benefits. Rather, an injured worker only needs to prove that the injury or illness was work-related. Nearly all employers are required to carry workers' compensation insurance in New York, and nearly all employees are entitled to collect WC benefits—including seasonal, temporary, part-time, and other types of workers who are less than full-time.

## WORKERS' COMPENSATION BENEFITS ARE LIMITED

The purpose of workers' compensation insurance is to provide a near-immediate source of funds to help an injured worker cover all necessary medical bills and a portion of your lost wages, but you only receive disability payments equal to two-thirds of your average weekly wage (multiplied by your percentage of disability) from the previous year's work up to a maximum of $1,063.05 per week in 2022.

For many construction workers, this leaves a significant gap in their household income. While you may also be entitled to other cash benefits in the event you suffer a permanent disability and are unable to return to work or cannot perform to the same level as you did prior to your accident, resulting in reduced earnings, these benefits are often not enough to make up for the economic loss from a construction accident. More important, WC benefits do not provide benefits for your pain and suffering or other non-economic damages.

The limited WC benefits available to injured construction workers include:

- Wage replacement up to two-thirds of your average weekly salary (subject to weekly cap – currently $1,063.05 per week in 2022)
- All reasonable medical costs related to your work accident
- Other cash benefits if you suffer partial or permanent disability
- No award for pain and suffering or other non-economic damages

Unlike a WC claim, a third-party claim allows an individual and his or her family to recover compensation for full lost wages as well as pain and suffering—which workers' compensation laws do not allow. As a result, individuals who are injured by a third-party will often recover more compensation than if they just filed a WC claim with the carrier.

## THIRD-PARTY CLAIM EXCEPTION TO WORKERS' COMPENSATION

Workers' compensation is said to be the "exclusive remedy" for injured workers. This means that a covered worker will need to go through workers' compensation insurance and gives up the right to sue their employer or coworkers who may have caused an accident resulting in injuries at work. There are, however, limited exceptions.

While you cannot sue your employer for work-related injuries absent rare circumstances, New York law permits you to bring what is called a "third-party claim" against other responsible parties (not a coworker or your employer) who caused your injuries. Due to the complex nature of New York Labor Law, it may be difficult to understand who may be a "responsible party."

## EXAMPLES OF THIRD-PARTY CLAIMS

Let's use an example of a worker who is employed by an electrical contractor on a construction site who may be injured by falling from a ladder. Even if the ladder was provided to the worker by his own employer, New York Labor Law §240(1) puts the responsibility of the worker's accident on the owner and general contractor of the jobsite if it is proven that the ladder was broken or was not the appropriate device for the task and the violation of the statute was a proximate cause of the accident. In such instance (and many others) even when a defective safety device is provided by a worker's own employer, the responsible party will be the owner and general contractor under New York Labor Law.

On a construction site, there are many other examples of when an injured worker may have a third-party claim. Some of the most common examples include the following:

- Motor vehicle accidents to and from the site caused by another driver, or on the construction site caused by another subcontractor's worker
- Forklift operator injures another worker from a different trade
- Another contractor's mistakes, such as a laborer slipping on a plumbing contractor's pipes that were dropped in a work area
- A stoneworker knocking over a gutter installer's ladder, or a roofer dropping debris on a siding installer
- Explosions or fires caused by a municipal or utility worker setting up lines
- The worksite owner not disclosing hidden dangers (i.e., a sinkhole or crack that could cause workers to fall),
- Many other defects that could result in serious personal injuries or the wrongful death of an innocent person
- Manufacturing defects in products like ladders, nail guns, lulls, and other devices

Due to the confusing nature of third-party claims in construction accidents, it is important to find an experienced and qualified NYC construction accident attorney who handles only accident cases and more importantly, one who understands the complexities of construction accidents and how New York Labor Law applies to your case.

CHAPTER 4

# WHO IS RESPONSIBLE FOR MY CONSTRUCTION ACCIDENT INJURIES?

## *SUING THIRD-PARTIES FOR YOUR CONSTRUCTION ACCIDENT INJURIES*

As mentioned in the previous chapter, workers' compensation insurance exists to protect employers from lawsuits when workplace injuries occur. In most cases, you cannot sue your employer after a construction accident, but you may have grounds for legal action against a third party. Seeking compensation for damages from a third party can make up the income not received from workers' compensation and address non-economic losses such as pain and suffering.

Sometimes it may be obvious who is responsible for your accident, but there are many accidents that may leave you confused about who, if anyone, you can sue for your injuries. The confusion is caused by the complex nature of New York Labor Law and the relationship between statutory liability and common law negligence of other contractors on site. Examples of third parties who could be partially or fully liable for injuries from a construction site accident include:

## PROPERTY OWNERS/ LEASEHOLDERS/OTHERS WITH OWNERSHIP INTEREST:

Many types of construction accidents are the responsibility of the construction site owner even if they were not actively negligent. Determining whether the owner is at fault depends on the type of work being performed and the manner in which the accident occurred. To workers, it may not seem obvious that an owner is at fault because the site owner may not be involved in the details of the work and/or may not be a presence on the jobsite at all.

However, the Labor Law recognizes that owners are in the best position to ensure a safe workplace. Therefore, in some cases where a worker falls from a height or an object falls on a worker (or other gravity-related accidents), an owner may be found 100% responsible for your injuries. For example, where a worker falls from a defective ladder provided by his own employer, the site owner may be found liable for your injuries under Labor Law §240(1) even though the owner had no involvement in the work performed or equipment provided.

In addition to statutory claims, property owners still bear the responsibility to maintain their property in a reasonably safe condition. This duty still applies when construction is ongoing. A property owner may be responsible for a slip and fall accident if they knew or should have known of a dangerous condition and failed to make it safe prior to an accident. An owner is also responsible if they exercise supervision and control over the means and methods of the work performed at the time of the accident under Labor Law §200.

## GENERAL CONTRACTORS:

Like owners, general contractors may be found liable for construction accidents involving falls from heights, falling objects or other gravity-related accidents pursuant to Labor Law §240(1). Similarly, general contractors may be responsible under Labor Law §241(6) when a violation of a specific and concrete Industrial Code provision is a proximate cause of a construction injury. General contractors also have an obligation to ensure the jobsite is reasonably safe. They must perform routine inspections and communicate with all subcontractors and their workers about any hazards or any dangerous conditions on the site as well as any dangerous activities. Similar to owners, a general contractor can be held liable if they exercise supervision and control over the means and methods of the work performed at the time of the accident under Labor Law §200.

## CONSTRUCTION MANAGERS/AGENTS:

Some projects include construction managers who typically act as an agent of the owner. Construction managers are not considered an "owner" or "contractor" as those terms are used in the Labor Law. Therefore, to hold a construction manager or other contractor liable as an agent of the owner or the general contractor, there must be a showing that the construction manager or other "agent" had the authority to supervise, control and direct the work that brough about the injury and the power to enforce safety standards. Whether a construction manager is liable for a construction accident under §200, §240(1) or §241(6) is case specific and requires an experienced construction accident lawyer to evaluate the role of a construction manager in the happening of the accident. A review of the contractual responsibilities of the construction manager as well as the absence of a general contractor may also be used in determining their liability under the Labor Law.

## OTHER CONTRACTORS/ SUBCONTRACTORS:

Other contractors (not your employer) and subcontractors are responsible for maintaining any area in which they work in a reasonably safe condition. A subcontractor can also be found liable if they control the work that caused your injuries. They can also be found vicariously liable for the actions/inactions of their employees while working in the course of their employment. Any negligence on the part of another contractor/ subcontractor and/or their employees can form the basis of liability in a construction accident. For example, if a plumbing contractor's employee drops pipes which fall on a laborer, the injured laborer can bring a third-party action against the plumbing contractor for the negligence of its employee.

## ARCHITECTS, ENGINEERS AND DESIGN PROFESSIONALS:

Construction jobs start in the planning stage and all projects require architects, engineers, land surveyors and other design professionals to conduct water and ground studies, land surveys, design plans of any structures and perform ongoing inspections throughout the project. Building codes, zoning ordinances and other safety rules and regulations must be adhered to during the entirety of the construction project. Any changes to the plans must be communicated to the general contractor and owner to ensure a safe workplace. If one of these design professionals fails to follow the proper codes, ordinances or accepted standards that result in a worker's injury, they may be a responsible party for a construction site accident. It should be noted, however, that Labor Law §240 and §241(6) exclude architects and engineers from liability unless actual negligence or direction and control over the work is established.

## EQUIPMENT MANUFACTURERS:

If your injury is caused by dangerous equipment or machinery, it may be due to a malfunction caused by either a manufacturing or design defect. These product liability claims, including failure to provide adequate safety warnings, would be brought against the designer, manufacturer and/or distributor of the defective equipment and/or machinery.

## EMPLOYER:

As mentioned previously, workers' compensation is the sole remedy against your employer in New York if your injury is caused by a coworker or your employer's negligence. However, in rare circumstances, such as if your employer intentionally caused your injuries or fails to carry workers compensation insurance in violation of law, you may bring a suit directly against your employer. In many construction accidents, however, there are other responsible third-parties that may be found liable for your injuries.

## OWNERS OF ONE AND TWO-FAMILY HOMES MAY BE EXEMPT:

New York Labor Law does not apply to owners of one and two-family homes who contract for, but do not direct or control the work. This exception was enacted to protect homeowners who, lacking business sophistication, may not know or anticipate the need to obtain adequate insurance to cover them against the absolute liability imposed by section 240(1). However, in limited circumstances an owner of a one or two-family dwelling who directs and controls the work may be found responsible for your injuries arising out of one of the protected construction activities discusses in Chapters 2. In addition, if a residential home is being used for commercial purposes, the exemption may not apply.

## IDENTIFYING ALL RESPONSIBLE PARTIES

As you can see, there are many potential third-parties who may be responsible for your construction accident injuries. While it is sometimes obvious who is responsible, it may be unclear at times, especially when owners and contractors may be found liable without any active negligence on their part, but instead, due to a statutory violation. An experienced construction accident attorney will investigate your accident to identify all responsible parties as early as possible to ensure you are compensated fully for your injuries.

CHAPTER 5

# HOW CONTRACTORS AND OWNERS DEFEND CONSTRUCTION ACCIDENT CASES

After your case begins by filing and serving a summons and complaint on the responsible party, their insurance company will hire a law firm to defend against your claims. The insurance company will throw as many legal arguments and defenses against you as possible. Of course, the defenses used by the carrier will depend on the type of construction accident claim you have. For example, in a Labor Law §240(1) claim, the focus will be on attacking the applicability of the statute to the accident or in claiming the worker was the sole proximate cause. Even if a defendant cannot establish a worker was the sole proximate cause, they will try to lower the amount of money they should pay for your damages by attempting to pass a portion of fault onto the injured worker or another responsible party whenever possible.

## HERE ARE SOME COMMON ARGUMENTS AND DEFENSES IN CONSTRUCTION ACCIDENT CASES

### THE ACCIDENT DID NOT OCCUR DURING A "COVERED ACTIVITY."

Owners, contractors and their insurers typically begin their fight by arguing that a construction accident does not qualify for protection under Labor Law §240 or §241(6). The initial focus is whether the activity performed at the time of the accident is listed in the statute as qualifying for its protection.

Specifically, a construction accident must involve one of the following "covered activities" in order to qualify for the protection of Labor Law §240(1):

- Erection
- Demolition
- Repair
- Alteration
- Painting
- Cleaning
- Pointing

A contractor, owner, and their insurance carriers will argue your work did not involve one of the above activities, thereby removing your accident from protection of Labor Law §240(1).

As examples, the tasks of inspecting and wallpapering are not specifically listed as covered activities. Any case in which a worker is injured while performing an inspection or in applying wallpaper, including accidents occurring while falling from a ladder or scaffold will be met with a defense that the inspection or wallpapering is not a covered activity.

These claims are typically decided on a case-by-case basis depending on the specific facts and the context of the work performed. A worker injured while performing an inspection or wallpapering (or other not specifically listed activities) may still have a viable Labor Law §240(1) claim if a worker can establish that the work being performed at the time of the accident was incidental to a covered activity or was part of a larger construction project.

## THE ACCIDENT DID NOT OCCUR ON A "STRUCTURE."

In order to qualify for protection under Labor Law §240(1), a gravity-related accident must occur on either a building or structure. While the definition of a building is essentially not in dispute, what qualifies as a "structure" is disputed by defendants at every opportunity. Under Labor Law §240(1), a "structure" is "any production or piece of work artificially built up or composed of parts joined together in some definitive manner."[4] The courts have opted in favor of an expansive view of what qualifies as a "structure" and have adapted a broad definition as necessary to bring all artificially built-up objects requiring scaffolding and other similar safety devices for the protection of

4 See Lewis-Moors v Contel of New York, Inc., 78 N.Y.2d 942, 943 (1991) quoting Caddy v Interborough R. T. Co., 195 N.Y. 415, 420 (1909).

workers. Nevertheless, defendants will argue an object or item is not a "structure" within the §240(1) statute whenever possible.

As examples, a "structure" may be something less substantial than a building. Courts have applied the term "structure" to include the following:

- Bridges
- Utility poles
- Ticket booths
- A crane
- Utility vans
- A pumping station
- A pipeline
- Sprinkler system attached to a cooling tower
- Garages
- A contractor's shanty
- Railroad car
- Shelving

Whether an item is a "structure" or not is generally determined on a case-by-case basis as it is dependent on the specific facts of a case. Some of the factors a court may look to in order to determine whether something is a structure include the item's size, purpose, composition, degree of complexity, the tools needed to construct it and/or dismantle it, and the amount of time it is intended to exist.

Some examples of items that courts have determined did not satisfy their definition of structure include temporary items such as a sign from a temporary exhibit suspended from a ceiling at a convention center. In addition, items in nature such as a tree generally do not qualify as they are not "artificially built up." Nonetheless, even work performed on these "non-structures" can still be protected if it can be established that the work was performed in conjunction with a larger project on a qualified structure. As an example, a worker who fell from a ladder while sawing a tree branch defeated a defendant's attempt to dismiss his §240(1) claim even though the tree was not a structure because the court determined the tree removal work was an integral part of a larger covered project on a home which qualified as a "building or structure."[5]

In the event a worker is injured while working on something that is not easily defined as a "structure", you can be sure that a contractor or owner will argue that Labor Law §240(1) does not apply to your case. An experienced construction accident lawyer will understand the complexities involved in determining whether an accident involves a "structure" thereby invoking the protection of the scaffold law.

## THE ACCIDENT DID NOT OCCUR IN THE CONTEXT OF CONSTRUCTION WORK COVERED UNDER §241(6).

The specific and concrete rules set forth in the Industrial Code for §241(6) claims that were discussed in Chapter 2 only apply to work in the context of specific types of work. For Labor

5 See Lombardi v. Stout, 80 N.Y.2d 296 (1992).

Law §241(6) claims, contractors and owners will argue your accident does not qualify for protection under the statute because the work you performed at the time of your accident is not considered one of the following types of work:

- Construction
- Demolition
- Excavation

Specifically, New York courts will dismiss a §241(6) claim if the work was not performed in the context of construction, demolition or excavation work. It is important to note, however, that liability under §241(6) is not limited to accidents on a building construction site. In order to determine whether your work is covered under §241(6), courts will look to the definition of "construction work" as defined by the Industrial Code:

> *"[a]ll work of the types performed in the construction, erection, alteration, repair, maintenance, painting or moving of buildings or other structures, whether or not such work is performed in proximate relation to a specific building or other structure and includes, by way of illustration but not by way of limitation, the work of hoisting, land clearing, earth moving, grading, excavating, trenching, pipe and conduit laying, road and bridge construction, concreting, cleaning of the exterior surfaces including windows of any building or other structure under construction, equipment installation and the structural installation of wood, metal, glass,*

> *plastic, masonry and other building materials in any form or for any purpose."* See 12 NYCRR 23-1.4 (b) (13).

It is therefore necessary for your lawyer to know what constitutes these three types of work and what does not qualify under the statute. If an owner, contractor or other responsible party can prove your accident did not occur while performing work in the context of construction work, you will lose the protection of Labor Law §241(6).

## THE ACCIDENT OCCURRED WHILE PERFORMING "ROUTINE" MAINTENANCE.

New York Labor Law does not provide protection for injuries that occur during routine maintenance, changing light bulbs, inspections, and other tasks considered "routine." As such, defendants will often argue a worker's activity at the time of their accident was "routine" and insufficient to be considered a "repair" or an "alteration" (covered activities) within the meaning of the Labor Law.

An experienced construction accident lawyer will understand the nuances involved in determining whether an activity is routine maintenance or significant enough to qualify as a repair, an alteration or other covered activity to bring it under the protection of the Labor Law.

The courts have held that the term "altering" requires, "making a significant physical change to the configuration or composition of a building or structure."[6] This definition excludes "routine maintenance" as well as "decorative modifications." The courts have further explained that whether a physical change is significant enough to be considered an alteration depends on its effects on the physical structure. As an example, a worker who falls while applying an advertisement to the face of a billboard could not establish a labor law claim as the work was not considered an alteration but only a decorative modification and did not change the billboard's structure. The work performed was also considered to be outside the construction context and merely the maintenance of a structure.[7] By comparison, a worker who falls while adding an extension to a billboard that changed the dimensions of the billboard frame in order to accommodate a new advertisement does constitute an alteration within the meaning of the Labor Law §240(1).[8]

The question of whether a particular activity constitutes a "repair" or "routine maintenance" is often determined on a case-by-case basis. In making this determination, courts will look at the complexity and scope of the work as well as whether the work involves the replacement of a missing, malfunctioning or worn-out component.[9]

For example, it has been held that the replacement or tightening of a screw in the arm of a nonmotorized door closer is merely routine and does not constitute repair work under Labor Law §240(1), while, in contrast, replacing the entire door track on a malfunctioning elevator constitute covered repair work.[10]

---

6 See Joblon v. Solow, 91 N.Y.2d 457 (1998).
7 See Munoz v. DJZ Realty, LLC, 5 N.Y.3d 747, 748 (2005).
8 See Saint v. Syracuse Supply Co., 25 N.Y.3d 117 (2015).
9 See Esposito v. New York City Indus. Dev. Agency, 1 N.Y.3d 526, 528 (2003).
10 See Thompson v. 1701 Corp., 51 A.D.3d 904 (2nd Dept. 2008).

Likewise, a worker who fell from a ladder while replacing a condenser fan motor on the roof of a store did not qualify for protection under §240(1) because the replacement of the motor was found to be the result of "normal wear and tear" and not "repairing" or any other covered activity under §240(1).[11]

Here are additional examples of work that has been deemed a qualified "repair" compared with work deemed to be unprotected routine maintenance:

| Qualified repair | Unprotected routine maintenance |
| --- | --- |
| Replacing light fixture on a parking lot pole | Changing burned out light bulb |
| Replacing transformer on roof's HVAC unit | Replacing boiler's defective safety valve |
| Replacing beverage supply line at restaurant | Replacing sign's power supply box |
| Replacing garage door opener | Adjusting loose chain on an overhead garage door |

As you can see, it can be difficult at times to discern between a qualified repair and unprotected routine work. These determinations are often made on a case-by-case basis depending on the factors listed above, including whether a smaller component is being replaced or an entire system needs replacement. An experienced lawyer will understand whether the work performed was substantial enough to qualify under these circumstances.

11 See Stockton v. H & E Biffer Enters. No. 2, LLC, 196 A.D.3d 709 (1st Dept. 2021).

## THE WORKER WAS NOT ENGAGED IN THE TYPE OF "CLEANING" THAT IS PROTECTED UNDER LABOR LAW §240(1).

Another covered activity under section 240(1) that is often in dispute is cleaning. While cleaning is a "covered activity" under the statute, what constitutes cleaning is not always clear. While it is settled law that workers injured while engaged in window washing commercial buildings are afforded protection for "cleaning" under the statute, outside of commercial window washing, New York courts have created a 4-prong-test to accidents occurring while cleaning. Specifically, any such work will not be covered under the statute if the task: (1) is routine, in that it is the type of job that occurs on a relatively-frequent and recurring basis as part of the ordinary care of a commercial premises; (2) requires neither specialized equipment or expertise; (3) generally involves insignificant elevation risks comparable to those encountered in typical domestic or household cleaning; and (4) is unrelated to any ongoing construction, renovation, painting, alteration or repair project. The courts have held that the presence or absence of any one factor is not necessarily dispositive, but that the court will view each case in its totality before determining whether it warrants the statute's protection. [12]

As an example, an employee of a commercial cleaning company hired to provide janitorial services for a retail store was not "cleaning" within the meaning of Labor Law §240(1) when he fell from a ladder while dusting a six-foot high display shelf. The task did not require specialized equipment or knowledge

12 See Soto v. J. Crew Inc., 21 N.Y.3d 562 (2013).

and the task was unrelated to a construction, renovation, painting, alteration or repair project.[13] In contrast, a worker who fell from a ladder while power washing an HVAC chiller was considered to be "cleaning" within the meaning of Labor Law §240(1) because the task was not routine as it did not occur on a recurring schedule, involved elevation risks not comparable to those encountered in domestic cleaning and it required specialized equipment. [14]

Any construction accident case involving cleaning, outside of window washing commercial buildings, will be met with strong opposition by owners, contractors and their insurance carriers. If you were injured while engaged in cleaning, make sure you and your attorney have a strong understanding of the 4-prong-test discussed above as early as possible in your case so that you can get the best outcome possible.

## RECALCITRANT WORKER AND SOLE PROXIMATE CAUSE.

As discussed in Chapter 2, if it is determined that Labor Law §240(1) was violated and the violation was a proximate cause of the accident, the owner and general contractor will be liable even if the worker may have contributed to the accident in some way. In fact, the court will simply ignore any potential negligence on the part of the worker under such circumstances. However, Labor Law §240(1) does not provide protection to a "recalcitrant worker" who deliberately refuses to use available safety devices resulting in injury. The recalcitrant worker defense is a practical application of the broader rule that when

13 See Soto v. J. Crew Inc., 21 N.Y.3d 562 (2013).
14 See Mazzarisi v. N.Y. Soc'y for the Relief of the Ruptured & Crippled, Maintaining the Hosp. for Special Surgery, 2022 NY Slip Op 2953 (1st Dept. 2022).

a worker's own actions are the "sole proximate cause" of his injuries, there can be no violation of the statute.

In order to succeed on a "recalcitrant worker" defense, it must be established that (1) the appropriate safety device was available; (2) the worker knew that the device was available and that he was expected to use it or was instructed to use it; (3) the worker chose not to use the device for no good reason or misused the device; and (4) the worker would not have been injured had they not made that choice.[15]

The "sole proximate cause" defense typically applies to accidents in which a worker deliberately misuses the proper equipment or the proper device was given to the worker and the worker decided not to use it or decided to use an inappropriate device, resulting in an injury. In such instance, there is no liability on the owner or general contractor under Labor Law §240(1).

For example, in a case where a worker was assigned a task which required him to climb approximately four feet to access a motor room, he chose to stand on an overturned bucket, instead of using a ladder which was available on the jobsite. The worker then attempted to exit the motor room by jumping down, thereby sustaining injuries. The New York Court of Appeals held that since ladders were available, the worker's normal and logical response should have been to get one. The worker's choice to use a bucket to get up and then to jump down on his own was the sole proximate cause of his injuries. He was not entitled to the protection of Labor Law §240(1). [16]

15 See Cahill v. Triborough Bridge and Tunnel Authority, 4 N.Y.3d 35, 40 (2004).
16 See Montgomery v. Federal Express Corp., 4 N.Y.3d 805 (2005).

In another case, a worker fell from an extension ladder while removing rust from the exterior of a window when the ladder retracted causing him to fall. He acknowledged that the ladder was steady and in good working order. He also revealed that he failed to lock the extension clips in place before climbing the ladder. The New York Court of Appeals made clear that when the proper safety device is provided and in place, there can be no violation of the statute. The worker's actions were the sole proximate cause.[17]

There have been many cases which appear to be very similar where liability may have been found in one case and not in the other. It is important that you find a construction accident attorney who is familiar with the Labor Law statutes as well as the many cases and judicial opinions that have interpreted the statutes in order to ensure you get the best possible outcome for your case.

## THE INDUSTRIAL CODE PROVISIONS ALLEGED TO HAVE BEEN VIOLATED DO NOT PROVIDE A SPECIFIC AND CONCRETE SAFETY STANDARD OR DO NOT APPLY TO THE FACTS OF YOUR CASE.

As mentioned earlier, Labor Law §241(6) claims require a violation of a specific and concrete safety standard set forth in the Industrial Code Rule 23. Contractors, owners and their insurance companies will argue any code provision you claim was violated simply restates general standards and does not set forth the necessary

17 See Blake v. Neighborhood Housing, 1 N.Y.3d 280 (2003).

specific standards needed for a valid §241(6) claim. Furthermore, they will argue the code provisions you cite that do require specific standards, nonetheless should be ignored because they do not apply to the facts of your case.

For example, a worker who trips and falls on debris may be faced with the defense that their §241(6) claim should be dismissed because the Industrial Code provision alleged to have been violated does not apply to the facts of their case. The closest applicable provision would be Industrial Code Rule 23-1.7 (e) (1) which requires passageways to be kept clear of debris or other obstructions which may cause tripping. However, these claims have been dismissed on occasion by defendants arguing the worker did not fall in a "passageway" but instead, in an open work area.

Likewise, Rule 23-1.7(e)(2) requires working areas to be kept clear of debris and "scattered tools and materials" insofar as may be consistent with the work being performed. This provision can potentially be defeated if the items that caused a worker to trip and fall are material used in the actual task the worker was performing at the time of the accident. For example, Rule 23-1.7(e)(2) did not apply to a worker who tripped on plywood which he was stacking at the time of his accident. The provision did not apply because the object on which the worker tripped was an integral part of the work he was performing.[18]

## COMPARATIVE NEGLIGENCE OF THE WORKER.

While Labor Law §240(1) does not allow a contractor or owner to claim that the construction worker was negligent and

18 Alvia v. Teman Electrical Contracting, Inc., 287 A.D.2d 421 (2nd Dept. 2001).

contributed to the accident once it has been established that a violation of the statute was a proximate cause of the accident, Labor Law §200 and §241(6) allow a defendant to point the finger at the injured worker and argue the worker was negligent in contributing to the accident, thereby reducing the amount of money they must pay in relation to the percentage of liability of the parties.

## NO SUPERVISION OR CONTROL OVER THE ACTIVITY THAT CAUSED THE WORKER'S INJURY UNDER A LABOR LAW §200 CLAIM.

In a "means and methods" claim pursuant to §200, owners and contractors will argue they are not liable because they did not exercise supervision and/or control over the activity that caused the injury. Typically, general supervisory authority to oversee a project is not enough. It must be established that an owner or contractor or their agent exercised their authority to supervise and control the work that brought about the injury.

## "SPECIAL EMPLOYEE"

As mentioned in Chapter 5, New York law provides that an employee who receives workers compensation benefits may not sue his or her employer in an action for personal injuries. In fact, this restriction has also been applied to prevent lawsuits against entities other than your employer when there is a "special relationship" between your employer (general employer) and the other entity (special employer).

In this regard, a general employee of one employer may be considered a special employee of another employer. The receipt of workers' compensation benefits from a general employer prevents an employee from suing a special employer. A "special employee" has been defined as "...one who is transferred for a limited time of whatever duration to the service of another. General employment is presumed to continue, but this presumption is overcome upon clear demonstration of surrender of control by the general employer and assumption of control by the special employer."[19]

A special employment relationship is not defined by one specific factor, but courts will often focus on who controls and directs the details and manner of the employee's work as well as who is responsible for the payment of the employee's wages, who has the power to discharge the employee and whether the work performed was in furtherance of the special employer's or general employer's business.[20]

In construction accident cases, a contractor or other responsible party may argue that an injured worker was acting as their "special employee" at the time of the accident. For example, Contractor A hires Subcontractor B to perform work on a project but Subcontractor B merely lends Contractor A its employees without providing any supervision or control over its employees' day-to-day-work while continuing to pay wages and workers compensation insurance for its employees. Contractor A is supervising, managing, directing and controlling the employees' work on a day-to-day basis, including all details of their work. If an employee of Subcontractor B is injured by falling off a defective ladder provided to him by Contractor A,

19 See Thompson v Grumman Aerospace Corp., 78 N.Y.2d 553, 557 (1991).
20 See Schramm v Cold Spring Harbor Lab., 17 A.D.3d 662 (2nd Dept. 2005).

the employee may be met with a "special employee" defense by Contractor A.

The worker's status as a special employee could prevent a claim for injuries under Labor Law §§200, 240(1), 241(6) and general negligence. It should be noted that whether a worker is a "special employee" is usually a question of fact for a jury, although this is not always the case, and may under certain facts, be decided as a matter of law by a judge.

It should also be noted, this "special employee" defense is not common and can only be claimed in certain circumstances as described above. However, it is important to find an experienced construction accident lawyer to evaluate your case early so that your outcome is as successful as possible.

CHAPTER 6

# THE LEGAL PROCESS IN A CONSTRUCTION ACCIDENT CASE

## *CONSTRUCTION ACCIDENT CASES SHOULD NOT BE SETTLED BEFORE FILING SUIT*

While some lawyers will try to settle a case before filing suit, I find that it is rarely worthwhile. If I agree to take a case, that means I have already decided to file suit. I will not waste time attempting to negotiate with an insurance carrier soon after an accident. There are several reasons.

First, since construction accidents rarely involve only minor injuries, our clients are still undergoing medical care. It is not wise to settle a case before your medical condition, including future prognosis, becomes clear. For some clients, this may occur in a few months. For others, it could take years. It would be foolish to wait to file suit for so long when the case can be moving through the court system instead. The New York City courts were already moving at a snail's pace. Unfortunately, the backlog of cases has gotten worse as a result of the covid-19 pandemic, thereby delaying cases further. It could take up to 4 years or more in several boroughs for your case to go to trial. Imagine if your lawyer waited 2 years to start the lawsuit because he or she wanted to try to settle the case pre-suit! I have seen some attorneys wait almost the entire three-year statute of limitations before filing suit. This is very dangerous. If an attorney sues the wrong property owner or other responsible party by mistake, your case will be dismissed.

Another reason I believe it is not worthwhile to attempt to settle a case pre-suit – the insurance companies do not offer fair settlements at such an early stage. Instead, they use the opportunity to gain as much information about you and your lawyer as possible to help them limit your recovery. If they see weakness, they will take advantage of you. An inexperienced lawyer can cost a client a fair settlement by settling for too little too soon.

It is only in a rare instance in which a client's injury is worth more than the defendant's insurance policy that I would settle a case pre-suit, and that would assume I have proof that the responsible party has no other insurance policies or has no assets. It must always be in the client's best interests in order to settle a case pre-suit.

## LITIGATION BEGINS WITH THE FILING OF A SUMMONS AND COMPLAINT

A lawsuit is started by filing and serving a summons and complaint. The person who files a lawsuit is called the plaintiff. The owner, contractor or other responsible party is called the defendant. The summons and complaint describe the legal basis for the claim against the defendant(s) and also sets forth facts that support the claim. After the lawsuit is filed, the defendant will serve an answer on the plaintiff. The answer will typically deny the allegations in the complaint and assert defenses and possible cross-claims against other defendants.

## DISCOVERY PROCESS

Both sides then participate in a process called "discovery" by asking for and exchanging information about the case, including each party's claims and/or defenses. The discovery process may involve requests for production of documents and other tangible materials that are relevant to the case, including exchanging witness information, photographs, daily construction logs, medical records, wage and attendance records, union and pension files, etc. The discovery process also includes depositions.

## DEPOSITIONS

A deposition is a face-to-face meeting where the attorneys are allowed to ask a witness questions under oath. Each party is required to appear for a deposition as well as other non-party witnesses who have relevant information about each party's claims and/or defenses. You will be required to answer questions about your personal background, education, skills, earnings, the accident, your medical care (including any prior treatment that may be related), as well as additional questions about your damages claim. The deposition is a very important legal proceeding, and an experienced construction accident lawyer will meet with you and prepare you multiple times before the deposition.

## PHYSICAL AND EXPERT EXAMINATIONS

The discovery phase also includes a request by the defendant that the worker appear for a medical exam by a doctor hired by the defendant's insurance company who will give an opinion on your injuries, causation, prognosis and permanency. In construction accident cases with significant injuries, it is not uncommon for you to undergo multiple medical exams by physicians in different specialties. For example, I have had clients who have been examined by an orthopedist for a shoulder injury, a neurosurgeon for a neck (cervical spine) injury as well as a physical medicine and rehabilitation doctor to provide an opinion on potential future medical needs - all in the same case.

In addition to medical exams, construction accident cases may also include vocational rehabilitation experts who administer a set of test questions and interview the worker to determine whether he or she is employable at some level based upon education, skills and physical and psychological abilities.

An experienced and qualified construction accident lawyer will never let you attend these exams alone. It is important to make sure these hired guns do not take advantage of a client by asking them inappropriate questions or to fill out extensive questionnaires or even lie about what occurred during an examination. While more inexperienced attorneys will often send clients to medical exams without an escort, thereby exposing the client to unknowingly hurt their own cases, a more experienced lawyer will use services that provide experienced professionals who can observe the exams, protect the client's rights and rebut any false claims about what occurred during the exam.

The discovery phase can take many months and sometimes more than a year. When it is completed, and each side knows what evidence will be offered at trial, the plaintiff will file a Note of Issue which alerts the court that the case is ready for trial.

## FILING A NOTE OF ISSUE AND MARKING A CASE TRIAL READY

Once a case is marked ready for trial by the filing of a note of issue, each side will have between 30 and 120 days (depending on the judge's individual rules) to file a motion for summary judgment. In construction accident cases, summary judgment motions are common as many construction accidents can be decided on the law rather than requiring a jury to decide questions of fact due to the prevalence of Labor Law §240(1) or §241(6) claims.

## SUMMARY JUDGMENT MOTION PRACTICE

The benefit of a plaintiff filing and winning a summary judgment motion on liability is that interest at 9% per year begins to run from the date the court issues its decision and a copy is provided to the defendant. This interest is important as it not only increases the ultimate value of your case (adding 9% per year to the final judgment), but it also puts pressure on owners, contractors and their insurance companies to settle the case sooner rather than later. Going to trial on damages only may take time due to court delays and the longer they wait, the more money they will be ordered to pay due to the accumulation of interest.

## COURT MANDATED SETTLEMENT CONFERENCES AND OUTSIDE MEDIATION

If the court issues an order in the worker's favor (and sometimes while a motion is being decided) the parties begin to discuss settlement of the case. This includes settlement conferences with the court or outside mediators. While most cases settle before trial, even in construction accident cases, some cases do go to trial after discovery has ended if the parties cannot come to an agreement. Sometimes my clients get nervous when I talk about "going to trial," or when I say things like "at trial." However, I believe that the best way to get a case resolved without going to trial is to thoroughly prepare for trial.

If an insurance company believes a lawyer is not prepared or is acting like the case will settle, the worker's lawyer is in a weak position to try to get a reasonable and just settlement offer for the client. Perhaps the most important decision you can make is the lawyer you hire for your construction accident case. Just as you want an experienced doctor treating you, you want an experienced trial lawyer handling your injury case. You don't want to hire a lawyer for a serious construction accident case only to find out a few weeks or months before trial that the lawyer has either never tried a case in court or that the lawyer is afraid to try the case.

## TRIAL

If the parties are unable or unwilling to settle their case during the discovery process or after motions are decided, the case will proceed to trial. In New York City, the trial process may differ slightly depending on which county your case is being litigated. Nevertheless, trials generally begin with jury selection and the assignment of a trial judge. Jury selection will usually be completed within one to two days, although sometimes it takes longer depending on the complexity of the case and availability of jurors. After jury selection, the case is conferenced with the trial judge to schedule witnesses and discussion of possible settlement. Assuming the case does not settle, the judge opens the trial with instructions to the jury, followed by opening statements from each side's attorney. Opening statements are intended to provide the jury with a clear picture of the claims asserted by the worker, the expected evidence that establishes the worker's claims and/or damages and sets forth an outline of what the jurors can expect. The trial proceeds with witness testimony, including direct and cross-examination of the parties and expert witnesses, together with trial exhibits such as copies of daily logs, safety meeting minutes, photographs and other documentary evidence and/or demonstrative exhibits. At the conclusion of testimony, the parties' lawyers begin closing arguments, highlighting the portions of trial they wish the jury to focus on. The judge then reads further instructions to the jury and provides them with a verdict sheet which consists of questions the jury must answer. The jury then begins deliberations and requests clarification of testimony or copies of exhibits if needed. The trial concludes with the jury's verdict. In New York, a construction accident jury trial (like other civil trials) consists of six jurors who deliberate and issue a final verdict. Typically, two alternate jurors are selected as a safeguard in the event a main juror becomes ill during trial or is otherwise unable to complete their service. Any alternate jurors remaining at the end of the closing arguments and the judge's final instructions are excused from jury duty as they do not deliberate with the other six jurors. A typical construction accident trial can take anywhere from a few days to a week or more depending on the complexity of the case and whether it is a full trial on liability and damages or a damages-only trial. Unlike a criminal trial, a civil trial does not require a unanimous verdict. Instead, each question the jury is required to answer must be agreed upon by at least 5 out of the 6 jurors, although it is not required that the same 5 jurors agree on every question. For example, it is sufficient for jurors 1-5 to agree on question 1 while jurors 2-6 agree on question 2, as long as at least 5 out of the 6 jurors agree in their answer to each verdict sheet question.

## FILING AN APPEAL

After a trial ends with a jury verdict, either side can file an appeal if they believe errors were made by the judge or the verdict was not consistent with the evidence. After the appeal is decided, sometimes the case may be returned to the trial court for further proceedings, including the entry of judgment as mentioned earlier.

## ENTERING JUDGMENT AND RECEIVING YOUR AWARD

Getting a jury verdict in your favor is not the end of your construction accident case. After a verdict, assuming there is no appeal, your lawyer must prepare and enter a judgment based upon the jury verdict. You will be entitled to 9% interest from the date of the verdict until the date the defendant issues payment. In addition, if you successfully won a summary judgment motion on liability before the trial, your interest would begin to run from the date summary judgment was granted. Sometimes, motions are granted years before the trial is held. A verdict in a plaintiff's favor can sometimes result in years of interest on top of the jury verdict.

CHAPTER 7

# WRONGFUL DEATH ARISING FROM A CONSTRUCTION ACCIDENT

DEALING WITH THE LOSS OF A LOVED ONE CAN BE ONE OF THE most difficult times of your life. When a family member's death was preventable and caused by the lack of proper safety precautions or the carelessness of another contractor, it can be even more overwhelming. While the last thing on your mind may be to call a lawyer, it is important to understand your rights and get the information and advice you need as early as possible.

## *WHAT IS A WRONGFUL DEATH LAWSUIT?*

Wrongful death is a death that is caused by someone's negligence or willful conduct. In the context of construction accidents, a violation of Labor Law §§200, 240(1) or 241(6) can also form the basis of a wrongful death lawsuit. In a wrongful death claim arising out of a construction accident, the worker's family can seek to recover for economic damages such as medical bills, funeral costs and loss of inheritance.

## WHAT IS A SURVIVORSHIP CAUSE OF ACTION?

A survivorship claim in New York is a cause of action that belongs to the estate of the deceased construction worker and not the beneficiaries. It is a claim for conscious pain and suffering which the deceased worker experienced from the time of the injury until death. Conscious pain and suffering claims are recoverable even if the victim was only conscious for seconds after an accident. Sometimes, experts are necessary to establish a timeline with regards to proving pain and suffering of a construction accident victim. Any award for conscious pain and suffering is distributed as part of the estate's assets pursuant to the deceased worker's will, or, if there is no will, then pursuant to New York intestacy law.

## WHO CAN FILE A WRONGFUL DEATH CLAIM IN NEW YORK?

A wrongful death claim is filed pursuant to the New York EPTL (Estates Powers and Trusts Law) and is brought by a personal representative of the estate. A wrongful death claim is brought on behalf of all the deceased worker's statutory beneficiaries, called distributees. Although who can recover as a distributee is defined by statute, generally, it is the surviving spouse, children or parent of the deceased worker. A survivorship claim is typically brought in the same action on behalf of the estate of the deceased person.

## DAMAGES IN A WRONGFUL DEATH CLAIM

Damages are intended to make a victim "whole" again. Unfortunately, in a wrongful death case, no amount of money can erase the tragic loss of a loved one. It is the hope that a recovery can assist a victim's family by alleviating the financial burden in a way the victim would have provided. The economic damages that are recoverable in a wrongful death case include:

- Healthcare expenses related to the decedent's final injuries
- Funeral costs and burial expenses
- Loss of financial support (based upon loss of expected wages)
- Loss of inheritance
- Loss of parental guidance
- Interest on the damages award from the date of death

The court will typically determine how an award for wrongful death is distributed among the beneficiaries as the distributions are not always the same depending on the individual relationship between the deceased person and each surviving family member.

# ARE PAIN AND SUFFERING AND EMOTIONAL DISTRESS RECOVERABLE IN A NEW YORK WRONGFUL DEATH CLAIM?

New York is one of only three states that does not allow surviving family members to recover for their own pain and suffering and emotional anguish for the loss of a loved one. The current law only provides for economic damages except in a very rare circumstance in which a surviving immediate family member was in the "zone of danger" at the time of the accident that caused the wrongful death. A zone of danger claim arises when a surviving family member is personally threatened with bodily harm and witnessed the injury or death of the victim. The "zone of danger" claim is generally not applicable in construction accidents as family members are typically not present at the scene of the accident.

In response to ongoing criticism of the current law, New York legislators have introduced a new bill called the Grieving Families Act. This bill would update current law and expand the damages allowed in a wrongful death claim to include damages for family members' emotional anguish caused by the wrongful death of a loved one, including loss of consortium, society and companionship. These mental anguish awards would be in addition to the current pecuniary loss already recognized. The proposed bill would also extend the statute of limitation for a wrongful death claim from 2 years to 3 ½ years from the date of death.

At the time of writing this book, the Grieving Families Act has not been made law and New York remains one of only 3 states that does not recognize surviving family members' right to recover for their own pain and suffering and emotional anguish for the loss of a loved one. Should you have questions about the status of this bill upon reading this book, please give us a call at 212-566-4868 and we would be pleased to provide you with an update on the current state of the law in this area.

## WHAT ARE THE TIME LIMITS TO BRING A WRONGFUL DEATH CLAIM IN NEW YORK?

Due to the complex nature of wrongful death law, it is important that family members contact an experienced wrongful death attorney as soon as possible. Many attorneys will simply tell you the statute of limitations in New York to bring a wrongful death claim is two years from the date of death. However, there is a different time limit for a survivorship claim for conscious pain and suffering which is sometimes overlooked by inexperienced lawyers. A survivorship claim must be filed within three years from the date of the injury which caused the death or one year after the death, whichever is later.

## SHORTER TIME LIMITS AND SPECIAL REQUIREMENTS FOR MUNICIPAL DEFENDANTS

Government entities have special requirements called "conditions precedent" that must be met in order to file a personal injury lawsuit in New York, including construction accident claims and wrongful death claims. A "notice of claim" is a document that must be served on the particular public entity as early as 90 days from the date the claim arose. A wrongful death notice of claim must be filed within *90 days of the appointment of a personal representative* of the estate. For a survivorship action, a notice of claim must be filed within *90 days of the accident which caused the death* of the construction worker.

Sometimes a personal representative of the estate may not be appointed for over a year. I have read about attorneys who mistakenly think they need to wait for the appointment of a personal representative to file both claims. This is not true. A notice of claim must be served as early as the first 90 days for a conscious pain and suffering claim. A separate or supplemental notice of claim can be served once a personal representative has been appointed for the wrongful death claim. It is best to hire an experienced attorney as soon as possible as these deadlines can be confusing.

To complicate things, the time limits for filing a lawsuit for these two related causes of action also differ when the wrongful death is caused by a municipal or public entity. In the context of construction accidents, the most likely public entities involved would be The City of New York and/or The New York City School Construction Authority, although any public entity involved as either a contractor or owner would trigger this shorter time period. A survivorship lawsuit against a public entity for pre-death conscious pain and suffering must be filed within *one year and 90 days from the date of the accident* which caused the death while the wrongful death lawsuit against a public entity must be filed within *two years from the date of death.*

CHAPTER 8

# 7 MISTAKES THAT CAN WRECK YOUR CONSTRUCTION ACCIDENT CASE

While some construction accidents can result in catastrophic injuries, it is important to remember that even if your accident does not result in serious injuries or you don't think you are seriously injured, you need to make sure you do a number of things after a construction accident as well as avoid some of the biggest mistakes that can wreck your case.

To the extent possible, try to have someone you trust obtain witness information and take photos of the accident scene, including the equipment that may have been involved in your accident – a ladder, scaffold, hoist or other equipment or any objects that may have fallen. If you tripped and fell on debris, ask a coworker to take photos of the debris.

The truth is that as soon as an injured worker is off the site, the owner and general contractor's representatives are immediately called to the scene to start taking photos and getting witness statements. Some investigators will even try to re-create (or stage) the accident scene to take photos of the way they want it to look. I had a case in which the general contractor's project manager picked up a ladder that had fallen and put it back in place before taking photographs.

Most construction sites consist of different trades at any one time. If you are injured while working on a construction site, there may be witnesses to your accident from another trade you do not know. It is important to obtain the contact information of any eyewitnesses to your accident immediately. Once you leave the site, this information may be lost forever as workers are often moved to different jobsites. If you obtain information at the time of the accident, it will be easier for your lawyer to seek out the witnesses for more detailed information.

Now that you know a few steps that can help your case, below are 7 of the biggest mistakes that can wreck your construction accident claim. Avoid these mistakes and give yourself a better chance at a successful outcome:

**1. Failing to report the accident immediately**

One of the most important things you must do after a construction accident is make sure you report it. If you were injured while working at a construction site, report it to your employer, union representative or general contractor/owner's representative on site immediately. Your employer is required to file a report of your accident with the Workers' Compensation

Board in order for you to obtain workers' compensation benefits. This will also ensure there is a record of your version of events. It also prevents the insurance carrier from denying the accident even happened which they will do if it was never reported or was reported late. This also provides an opportunity to make sure the contractor and owner preserves any evidence, including possible video of the accident or the equipment that may have caused your accident. If you fail to report the accident immediately, vital evidence could be lost.

**2. Providing a written or recorded statement or signing an accident report prepared by someone else before you have been examined by a medical professional.**

Oftentimes, construction sites will have a medical trailer or safety office onsite. After an accident, the injured worker may be escorted to this office and asked questions about the accident before being sent to a local hospital or medical office. Injured workers are often instructed to sign an accident report even before you're taken to a doctor and may even be asked to sign a statement written by someone else. Even more offensive, you are asked questions and your answers are being audio recorded!

I don't think it is wise to sign any forms before getting yourself examined by a medical professional. After an accident you may not be thinking clearly, your adrenaline may be high, masking your pain and clouding your perceptions. You could also be suffering a concussion. No one on site is looking out for your well-being if you are being asked to sign your name to an accident report before getting medical care.

In addition, injured workers are often contacted shortly after an accident by a private investigator on behalf of the owner, developer or general contractor and want to get a statement from you about how the accident happened. These investigators are looking out for the insurance company as well as the owner and contractor and are solely focused on blaming you for your injuries. I suggest you speak to an attorney who has experience in construction accident cases first before giving any statements whether written or verbal.

**3. Waiting too long to seek medical treatment or having too long a gap in care.**

Even if you don't think you are seriously injured, it is important to get medical treatment as soon as possible. As mentioned earlier, after an accident, your adrenaline is high and this can sometimes mask your pain, making it difficult to assess your own physical condition. You also may not be thinking clearly and your judgment may be clouded. If you don't seek medical attention immediately, you provide the insurance companies with their favorite argument – that your injuries were not serious since you didn't even go to the hospital or doctor on the day of the accident. When you seek medical treatment immediately after the accident, it also documents the accident and your complaints of pain close in time to the accident. Make sure you express all your complaints after the accident, even if you believe them to be minor. Insurance companies will dispute that your injuries were caused by your construction accident if you did not seek medical care soon after an accident or made no complaints on your initial visit.

Also, make sure that you, or a friend or family member, call for an ambulance if you feel that your injuries are serious. I have had clients get injured, some very seriously, and the owner or contractor tries to hide the serious nature of the accident by sending the worker to a doctor's office or urgent care facility in a co-worker's car or taxi. I even had a case in which a contractor made my client walk 7 blocks to a local medical office with a coworker to prevent a record of the seriousness of the accident. Even more egregious, I handled a case in which the worker did not speak English and the contractor's representative personally drove the worker to a hospital in another borough and proceeded to act as translator and falsely reported that the accident did not occur on the jobsite! Property owners and contractors oftentimes are more concerned with finishing a project ahead of schedule and under budget than the safety of their workers.

**4. Failing to follow doctor's advice.**

While you need to follow-up with medical appointments and listen to doctor's advice, you also don't want to wreck your construction accident case by failing to follow up with treatment, since that will give the insurance company another argument against you at trial. A typical defense lawyer's closing argument in such a situation would be "What do people do when they don't feel well? They go to the doctor. When was the last time the plaintiff went to the doctor? Two years ago! I guess he must be feeling better." Don't miss appointments, take your medication, do the exercises you're shown, and follow the treatment plan. Medical care provides a way to measure your injuries and acts as evidence that your injuries are for real. Make sure you reschedule an appointment if you cannot make it. I have seen client's medical records where multiple entries read, "Failed to show." This never looks good for your case.

5. **Not being truthful about past accidents or exaggerating your injuries.**

You are not helping your case by hiding past injuries from your lawyer or your treating doctors. You may not think it is important to mention a past accident or injury because you have recovered or it was many years earlier; however, an insurance company will use your denial as ammunition against your credibility. The insurance companies have access to databases and will already know your prior history. They will only ask you the question to test your credibility and if you don't admit it, you could damage your case. You can still have a claim for injuries even if you had a prior injury. Of course, you are only entitled to compensation to the extent the at-fault party made your injury worse. But you can still recover damages for your losses.

Likewise, exaggerating your injuries will not help your claim. In all injury cases, the insurance company will hire its own doctor to examine you and write a report with an opinion as to your injuries--whether they were caused by the accident, whether you have fully recovered or require future medical care. While these reports look the same in many cases (because the insurance companies continue to use the same "experts") you should be careful to not exaggerate your injuries, as some tests can clearly expose any exaggerations, potentially hurting your case.

Insurance companies also routinely hire private investigators to conduct video surveillance. If you are suffering from a serious back injury and you testified at a deposition that you are confined to your home and cannot engage in any meaningful physical activity, you better not be caught climbing ladders, cleaning gutters or carrying 50-pound bags of mulch into your backyard. These exaggerations could ruin your case.

**6. Posting pictures and videos and discussing your case on social media.**

In today's world, it is second nature to post photos and video of what's going on in your life. It is a way to keep in touch with friends and family. It is also a way to wreck your construction accident case. One of the first steps insurance companies take after an accident is reported to them is to search social media platforms for information on you. If you typically use social media to keep in touch with others, you may feel it's normal to let them know about your accident and how your injuries are coming along. Insurance companies are looking for anything you say to use against you. Any comment that "you're doing ok" or "you will be fine" to others will be used against you to minimize your injuries and devalue your case.

Posting photos of you enjoying yourself at the beach or at a party can potentially hurt your case. Even if there's no video of you dancing or swimming, the posts will undermine any argument that you're unwell or unable to enjoy life. Of course, these photos don't explain that you were only there for a few minutes just to say hi or that you may have been taking pain medication so you could make the trip to see friends. Instead, insurance companies will argue these photos are evidence that you don't deserve any compensation as you're not that seriously injured.

Also don't accept friend requests from people you don't know. Private investigators hired by insurance companies have been known to pretend they are someone they're not in an effort to get information about you to hurt your case. Don't post photos of physical activities even if they are old photos. These can be a headache to explain if the photos you posted after the accident are actually events that occurred prior to your accident. Finally, check your settings to make sure your account is private.

7. **Not speaking to an experienced construction accident lawyer as soon as possible.**

If you delay speaking with an experienced construction accident attorney, you are hurting your case. First of all, if you wait too long you could miss the time limit to bring a case, especially if a public entity is involved. In addition, evidence may be lost, witnesses may have moved and your memory may not be as detailed. If you hire a qualified attorney as soon as possible they can spot potential problems or anticipate defenses early on and can help you avoid mistakes or at least minimize them.

After a construction accident, you will also need to notify your employer within 30 days of the accident and file a workers' compensation employee claim form as soon as possible in order to begin receiving workers' compensation benefits. While you may feel that you are capable of filing a claim on your own, it is always useful to speak with an attorney before filing any legal paperwork.

Because workers' compensation benefits are limited in scope and do not fully compensate you for your injuries, a third-party action against another responsible party not your employer can provide additional compensation to make you whole. An experienced construction accident lawyer will evaluate all aspects of your claim and determine whether you have a valid third-party claim against the site owner, contractor or other responsible party. The sooner you contact a qualified construction accident lawyer, the earlier an investigation can begin to provide the best outcome possible.

Call us at 212-566-4868 or 718-948-3500 if you have additional questions about your construction accident case or other injury questions.

CHAPTER 9

# DETERMINING THE VALUE OF A CONSTRUCTION ACCIDENT CASE

THERE IS NO MAGIC FORMULA BY WHICH SOMEONE CAN PREDICT with certainty the amount of money that a construction accident case may be worth soon after an injury. Any lawyer that provides a specific number value at a first meeting is either not experienced enough to evaluate your claim or is simply telling a prospective client what they want to hear.

The value of your case depends on multiple factors that can vary from case to case and client to client. These factors can change over time as a case moves through the litigation process, making any such prediction even more unreliable at such an early stage.

Injury cases involving construction workers can be even more difficult when it comes to determining a value because construction accidents often cause catastrophic or life-altering injuries that may result in the inability to return to work and earn a living. However, sometimes, the injuries may not seem severe enough to prevent you from returning to your job. Estimating the impact of an injury on future employment can be highly speculative in the very beginning of a case because maximum medical improvement has not yet been attained and the full extent of the injuries are not fully known.

An experienced construction accident attorney will try to provide you with a range of settlement values as the case proceeds and some of the issues in your case become clearer. It should be noted that the settlement value of a case is typically less than the verdict a jury may render. The settlement value takes into account the enormous expense and risk of going to trial. The settlement is a certainty. The verdict is a risk.

Many factors influence the value of a construction accident case:

- The extent and severity of the worker's injuries
- Establishing a violation of Labor Law §§240(1), 241(6) or 200 as well as the degree of negligence of a defendant in a non-statutory claim
- The type, extent, and frequency of medical treatment
- The need for future medical care
- The parties' likeability and credibility
- The worker's age
- Work-life expectancy tables as well as life-expectancy tables

- Scarring or disfigurement
- Medical expenses (past and future)
- The client's ability to work in the future
- The specific legal issues involved in the case
- The county or venue where the case will be filed
- The dollar amount of settlements and verdicts for
- Similar types of cases in the past
- The insurance coverage available

An important factor that is sometimes ignored is the actual amount of money available to compensate a worker for their injuries. Contractors, owners and other responsible parties carry liability insurance to cover an injury claim. In a perfect world, there would be unlimited insurance to cover the full amount of your damages. Unfortunately, some defendants may have limited insurance coverage. In these rare circumstances, the insurance available is not sufficient to compensate an injured worker for the full amount of their damages.

For example, a construction worker in his 30's earning $100,000/year may have sustained life-altering injuries preventing any future employability. If the owner, contractor or other responsible party only has a $1million policy, the future earnings loss alone will exceed the amount of coverage available, leaving the injured worker undercompensated for his pain and suffering and other economic losses. Unfortunately, in these rare cases, the amount of insurance coverage will ultimately dictate the highest amount realistically recoverable irrespective of the true "value" of the case.

It is also important to understand that no two cases are alike, even if the construction accident causing the injuries and the injuries themselves are nearly identical. The evaluation of two construction accident cases that appear to be similar on the surface may produce widely different results due to the other factors listed above. For example, let's look at two 42-year-old electricians who fall from a ladder sustaining a left shoulder rotator cuff tear, and C3-4 and C4-5 cervical disc herniation injuries:

| Worker 1 | Worker 2 |
|---|---|
| Age 42 | Age 42 |
| Salary $125,000/year | Salary $125,000/year |
| Cervical discectomy and fusion surgeries | Cervical laminectomy surgery |
| Left shoulder arthroscopic repair rotator cuff with physical therapy | Left shoulder physical therapy treatment only |
| Unable to return to work | Missed 18 months of work |
| Bronx, NY | Staten Island, NY |

While Worker 1 requires surgery for the shoulder, Worker 2 recovers after only physical therapy for the same shoulder injury. With regards to the same cervical injuries, Worker 1 undergoes a significant surgical procedure limiting his range of motion, while Worker 2 undergoes a more limited surgical procedure that does not limit his range of motion. Last, Worker 1 is no longer able to return to work resulting in future lost earnings and other economic loss while Worker 2 missed 18 months from work but does not have any future lost earnings. Despite the same age, same job, same salary and same injuries, Worker 1 has a higher value case due to the differences in required treatment, physical recovery, future losses and other factors discussed above.

Evaluating construction accident cases takes a lot of knowledge, experience, and some seasoned intuition. Without these traits you may be at a serious disadvantage when negotiating with the insurance adjuster. And unless you are in the business of evaluating and settling construction accident cases for a living, you should look to an experienced injury lawyer for guidance.

## HOW DAMAGES ARE DETERMINED IN A CONSTRUCTION ACCIDENT CASE

Part of determining the value of a construction accident case involves an analysis of the damages claim. Damages in a construction accident case are intended to "make the plaintiff whole" or put the worker back in the same position they were in before the accident. Unfortunately, the only way our legal system can attempt to do this is by providing for a monetary award to compensate for the damages caused by a contractor, owner or other responsible party's actions.

As mentioned above, each construction accident case is unique, each worker is different, and as each injury can affect each worker differently, the damages in each case may be different.

Each case begins with an analysis of a worker's past pain and suffering. This category is intended to compensate for the pain, suffering and loss of enjoyment of life from the date of your accident until the date of the verdict. Injured workers with permanent injuries are also entitled to claim future pain and suffering which is intended to compensate you for the pain, suffering and loss of enjoyment of life from the date of the verdict until the end of your life expectancy which is determined by life expectancy tables.

Other damages recoverable in construction accident cases include medical expenses, lost wages, loss of future earning capacity, lost pension benefits, and lost fringe and other health benefits. The facts of each individual case will determine the damages that any particular worker is entitled to receive in order to make them whole again.

| Types of Damages in a Construction Accident Case | |
|---|---|
| Past Pain and Suffering | Future Pain and Suffering |
| Past Medical Expenses | Future Medical Expenses |
| Past Lost Wages | Future Lost Wages |
| Emotional Trauma | Pension and/or Union Benefits |
| Mental Anguish | Social Security Retirement Benefits |
| Loss of Enjoyment of Life | Loss of Consortium |

In fact, in construction accident cases, your past medical bills were likely paid for by the workers' compensation carrier which will demand reimbursement for a portion of the payments made for your medical care and lost wages. You will need to claim as damages your past medical expenses and wages so that you can satisfy the workers' compensation lien at the end of your case.

In addition to past medical expenses, some workers will also claim as damages future medical expenses if there is evidence that future care is necessary. You may also be entitled to past as well as future lost wages. If you are a union worker or government employee, you could be entitled to future lost pension benefits, fringe benefits, including health care benefits. Lastly, if there is evidence presented that you are unable to return to work, you also may also be entitled to lost future social security retirement benefits.

Construction accidents usually require experts to assist in calculating the value of your case. A life-care planner is an expert who will review your medical records and develop a plan of care that will cover the remainder of your life expectancy and itemize all medical care that is expected to treat your injuries that were caused by the accident. A life-care plan could include monthly prescription costs, visits to doctors, physical therapy sessions, x-rays, MRIs, even surgery and post-surgery therapy, as well as possible home health aides in your later years.

An economist is another expert that may be needed to calculate your future economic loss. An economist will use the information provided by other experts to calculate the future value of your economic loss so that a jury can determine an award for damages that considers your expected work life as well as your life expectancy. While your future lost earnings are based upon your wages at the time of your accident, an economist will explain to a jury that as we get older, we get raises and promotions and our salaries increase. Economists also calculate for the cost of inflation to determine your complete future lost earnings as well as the cost of medical care in your later years, as the cost of surgery or even physical therapy will likely be more expensive in 10-20 years than it is now.

CHAPTER 10

# FREQUENTLY ASKED CONSTRUCTION ACCIDENT QUESTIONS

When I meet with potential clients during a free consultation, I find that they have many of the same concerns. I want to provide a brief sample of the types of questions that are asked as these may be some of the same questions that you may have now. I want to educate you and provide a further understanding of the legal process to better prepare you before you meet with a lawyer about your case.

## *WHAT HAPPENS DURING A FREE INITIAL CASE REVIEW?*

During a free case review a lawyer will ask you about the facts of your accident. It is important to provide as much information as possible. You should bring any papers, documents or photos relevant to your claim, including any accident reports, medical records and witness names. It is important that you be upfront with your lawyer about any past injuries. In order to properly assess a case, an attorney needs as much information as possible. Remember that any consultation is confidential and will stay between you and the attorney. It is important to be truthful and not hide any information you feel may hurt your case. Of course, you should also ask the attorney any questions you may have about their experience in cases similar to yours as well as any other questions you may have in order to make the best decision possible for you and your family.

## WHAT ARE THE TIME LIMITS FOR FILING A CONSTRUCTION ACCIDENT LAWSUIT FOR INJURIES IN NEW YORK?

In New York, an injury victim has three (3) years to bring a claim for injuries arising out of someone's negligence such as a construction accident. However, if a claim is against a municipal entity (such as The City of New York), the time limit is much shorter. The City of New York may be a defendant in some construction accident cases as the City is involved in many construction projects as an owner. For municipal entities such as this, you must file what is called a "notice of claim" within 90 days of the date the claim arises. The notice of claim provides the municipal entity with information about the date, time and place of the occurrence as well as the manner in which the accident occurred and a description of the injuries claimed. It permits the municipal entity the opportunity to investigate the claim in a timely manner. You then have 1 year and 90 days from the date the claim arises to start the lawsuit by filing a summons and complaint.

**Be careful** - the New York City School Construction Authority, which is a separate municipal entity from the City of New York, is also involved in many City construction projects and has an *even shorter one-year statute of limitations* within which you must start your lawsuit by filing a summons and complaint, provided that you filed a timely notice of claim.

## WHAT IS A "CONTINGENCY FEE" AND HOW DOES A CONSTRUCTION ACCIDENT LAWYER GET PAID?

Most construction accident lawyers who accept cases in New York will handle your case on a "contingency" basis. This means that any fee recovered is contingent on getting you compensation by settlement or verdict. You do not need to pay the lawyer until and unless the lawyer wins your case. If an attorney does not win your case, you pay nothing.

The contingency fee system helps put injury victims on even footing with large insurance companies who have unlimited funds to pay defense attorneys to fight legitimate claims. Injured victims can now hire a very experienced attorney to fight for them without having to worry about the bill for legal services. Many injury victims would not be able to have their cases heard and would be forced to accept whatever lowball offer an insurance company wishes to make.

In New York, most personal injury attorneys handle accident cases pursuant to a 33 1/3 percent contingency fee agreement. All fee agreements must be in writing. You should also know that the contingency fee does not include the expenses that accrue during the course of your case. For example, the cost of medical records, court filings, expert fees, court reporter fees and other out-of-pocket expenses are the responsibility of the client. However, many injury lawyers do not bill the client for these expenses in the event money is not recovered. Make sure you ask your attorney about their policy on expenses and that such policy is in the written retainer agreement.

## HOW LONG WILL MY CASE TAKE?

The answer is "it depends" because each client's case is different; it is not a simple answer. While some clients may wish for their cases to be settled quickly, this is not usually the best way to resolve a case. You should be cautious of any attorney that promises to settle your case quickly as such a lawyer likely does not have the experience required to handle a construction accident case. It is never a good idea to attempt to settle a case before you have reached your maximum medical improvement, which is the time when your medical condition has stabilized and we know exactly what type of future medical care, if any, you will need. Sometimes, your injuries may require surgery that will result in recovery times that vary. Some clients may recover in a few months; for others, it could take a few years. Another factor that some lawyers don't acknowledge is that *where* your case is filed also becomes a factor. For instance, in New York City, cases in Bronx County take longer to finish than cases in Staten Island simply because there are many more cases filed in the Bronx and not enough judges to handle them. Last, at the time of writing this book, due to the Covid-19 pandemic, the New York City court system has been unusually slow in resolving cases due to the limit on jury trials, thereby exacerbating the typical delays occurring in various counties.

## CAN I BRING A CONSTRUCTION ACCIDENT LAWSUIT IF I WAS PARTIALLY AT FAULT?

As discussed in Chapter 2, if the court determines that a violation of Labor Law §240(1) occurred and the violation was a proximate cause of your injuries, there can be no comparative fault on the worker's part (even if there was some evidence that a worker may have been partially at fault).

In a §200 and/or §241(6) case where it is determined that you were partially at fault, you are still entitled to recover for that portion of your injuries that is attributable to another party or multiple parties depending on the facts of your case.

To explain, if a case is not settled prior to trial or a judge has not ordered summary judgment in your favor as a matter of law, a jury will be asked whether the defendant violated Labor Law §200, §241(6) or was negligent and whether the defendant's violation/negligence was a cause of the accident. If the jury answers "yes" to both questions, they will then be asked whether you, the plaintiff, was also negligent and a cause of the accident. If they say "yes" to both, the jury is then asked to determine the percentage of fault of each of the parties in causing the accident. Then they are asked to determine the damages – that is, the worth of your case. So, if the jury determines your case is worth $3 million, and you are found 50% at fault – you would be entitled to recover 50% of the verdict or $1.5 million. This is the percentage of fault attributable to the defendant(s). Even if you are 90% or more at fault in New York, you would still be entitled to recovery the remaining 10% of the verdict. In some states, like Virginia, you may not recover anything if you are even just 1% at fault for an accident.

## CAN AN UNDOCUMENTED WORKER BRING A CLAIM FOR CONSTRUCTION ACCIDENT INJURIES?

New York law provides the same rights to undocumented workers who are injured while working on construction sites as U.S. citizens and authorized immigrant workers. Some employers try to take advantage of their workers' immigration status to discourage them from applying for workers' compensation benefits or even consulting with a lawyer about their legal options. Some contractors may even try to scare undocumented workers with deportation or threaten to fire them if they report their accident. Under New York law, employers are not permitted to threaten or retaliate against their employees who file for workers' compensation benefits, a personal injury lawsuit or report workplace safety violations. It is important to ask questions and understand your rights if you are an undocumented worker and you've been injured in a construction accident. Undocumented workers are entitled to bring these claims. If you fear deportation for seeking compensation for your construction accident injuries, call us to protect your rights.

CHAPTER 11

# HOW TO CHOOSE THE RIGHT ATTORNEY FOR YOUR CONSTRUCTION ACCIDENT CASE

## *HOW DO I FIND THE RIGHT ATTORNEY FOR MY CONSTRUCTION ACCIDENT CASE?*

Choosing the right attorney for your construction accident case is an important, but sometimes difficult task. You must take your time and evaluate your choices. Mistakes made early in a case can have devastating consequences later. Early and proper investigations can make the difference if the case proceeds to trial.

The decision should not be based upon lawyer advertising alone. Just because a firm buys lots of advertising does not mean it hires good lawyers – just good advertisers! These "settlement mills" are firms that handle hundreds of cases at a time and look to settle them quickly, sometimes for pennies on the dollar, and move on, looking for more money to buy more advertising. These firms often do not know you or your case and will have your file handled by a young attorney with little experience. If a case needs to be tried, they often don't have the experience or skill needed and will instead look to refer that case to someone like me. The insurance companies know who these lawyers are and so should you.

In fact, according to a 2009 article in *The Georgetown Journal of Legal Ethics*, "*Run-of-the-Mill Justice*" by Nora Freeman Engstrom, (Vol. 22:1485) settlement mill law firms work because the insurance industry likes them.

The article explains the insurance industry's cooperation with settlement mill law firms. The reason is simple – it's profitable for them. Insurance companies get to save their money by paying out pennies on the dollar against high value claims. Settlement mills are willing to sell out their clients for fast money because they also get to settle other small "soft tissue" cases that would ultimately be thrown out of court as frivolous. Unfortunately, the losers in this scheme are the individuals with serious injuries who unknowingly settle their claims for a fraction of their true worth. Please do not be fooled by these types of attorneys.

Other firms advertise that they handle personal injury cases as well as family law, bankruptcy, criminal defense, etc. I call these lawyers "general practitioners." Personal injury law, and more specifically, construction accident law is too nuanced for lawyers who do not focus their practice solely on injury cases.

Insurance companies know which lawyers will go to court and try a case to verdict and who will not. These general practitioners do not have the experience to get their clients a fair settlement as a lawyer who solely handles injury cases.

Get a referral from an attorney you may know, even if they don't handle personal injury cases. He or she will likely know an attorney who focuses on personal injury law and has experience with construction accident cases. I often try to refer callers who need a lawyer in an area of law that I do not practice.

Be careful of any lawyers who try to rush you into signing a retainer agreement until you are ready. All of your questions should be answered and any concerns addressed. You can always ask to take the agreement home first to read it before making your decision.

Do not hire an attorney who contacts you in person or via telephone before you have reached out to them first. It is against the ethics code for attorneys to solicit clients this way without some type of initial contact by the injured person unless the recipient is a close friend, relative, former client or existing client. Likewise, do not hire an attorney based upon a referral from a doctor's office or hospital staff member or anyone else you don't personally know.

Beware of runners. These are scammers who approach you at the accident scene or the hospital emergency room or even in your doctor's waiting room. They are called runners because they are paid by unscrupulous lawyers to run to accident scenes and emergency rooms. I am disgusted by this behavior; lawyers are not permitted to do this.

# FINDING A QUALIFIED CONSTRUCTION ACCIDENT ATTORNEY

Here is a further list of some qualifications as well as some questions to think about before finding the right lawyer for your case:

1. **What type of experience do they have with your type of case.** The longer they have practiced personal injury law, the more they know. Look for lawyers who have handled construction accident cases in the past. Experience can be an important factor in winning your case.

2. **Do they have experience actually trying cases?** Insurance companies know the lawyers who never try cases and the ones that have done it before and are willing to do it again. Make sure your attorney has actually tried cases to verdict.

3. **Do they have a list of verdicts and settlements for construction accident cases?** Do not accept that their results are confidential. –If this is their response, they have nothing good to share with you. An attorney should still be able to share case information without revealing confidential names.

4. **Do they have testimonials from clients and other attorneys who practiced in their local area?** Another sign that a lawyer is experienced and qualified to handle a serious personal injury case is whether he or she has endorsements from other attorneys as well as client testimonials.

5. **Ask about their client communication policy and who will be handling your case.** Some offices will have the lead partner meet with you during your initial consultation and then after you sign a retainer agreement – you never speak with that attorney again. Instead, you are handed off to case managers, paralegals or inexperienced attorneys. Who will handle your depositions or a trial if necessary? At the O'Connor Law Firm, I am the attorney who handles a client's case at every turn.

6. **Can the attorney provide you with how they handle the legal process for your type of case in writing, including what you can expect as one of their clients.** Make sure that the attorney explains how he or she plans to handle your case, including explaining the steps involved in moving your case forward.

7. **Ask for proof that the attorney carries malpractice insurance.** This is a must and do not accept no for an answer: I am still amazed when I hear stories about lawyers without insurance.

8. **Do they have information like this book or a website so you can find out about their qualifications, experience and method of handling cases.** Always try to learn as much about an attorney as you can. Written materials are a great way to learn about an attorney and determine whether they are organized, focused and serious about handling your claim.

9. **Peer recognition** – Has the lawyer obtained peer recognition for their work. Are they a member of the Multi-Million

Dollar Advocate Forum, The National Trial Lawyers Top 100 Trial Lawyers, rated *AV Preeminent* by Martindale-Hubbell, or rated by SuperLawyers?

10. **Do they hold membership in trial lawyer associations.** In New York City, there are several organizations that most true trial lawyers will belong to – including the New York State Trial Lawyers Association (NYSTLA), NYS Academy of Trial Lawyers and the American Association for Justice (AAJ). Membership in these organizations demonstrates their commitment and dedication to personal injury trial law. These organizations also provide extensive education and networking to keep trial lawyers on top of the issues that affect their practice. They are also dedicated to fighting for the rights of injury victims by advocating for new legislation and preventing tort reform efforts by the insurance companies in our state.

11. **Publications** – Has your attorney written anything that has been accepted for publication on personal injury or construction accident law. This is another indication of his or her skills, authority and experience.

## ONCE YOU HAVE DECIDED ON AN ATTORNEY MAKE SURE YOU BOTH UNDERSTAND YOUR GOALS AND YOU UNDERSTAND HOW THE RELATIONSHIP WILL WORK

How will your attorney keep you informed about the progress of your case? At The O'Connor Law Firm, we keep in close contact with our clients to monitor their recovery, make sure they are getting the medical care they need and ensure we have all the documentation necessary to prove how their lives have been affected. We also provide a blueprint of the legal process as well as the timeframe each stage will take. We encourage our clients to call us anytime they have questions or concerns about their case. If I am in court on trial or in depositions, I will return your call as soon as I am available. Our clients are also invited to make an appointment to come into our office to discuss their cases at any time.

Find out who will be handling your case. Make sure there are no misunderstandings on this issue. Some firms will have a partner meet the client at the initial consultation. After signing a retainer agreement, the partner is never seen again, replaced by a younger attorney with little experience. If you retain a law firm because you want a specific lawyer to handle your case, make sure that person is going to be handling your case.

CHAPTER 12

# WHAT CAN A QUALIFIED CONSTRUCTION ACCIDENT ATTORNEY DO FOR ME?

If you have carefully read the previous chapters about the legal requirements for proving Labor Law §§200, 240(1) and 241(6) claims, as well as the many ways owners and contractors attempt to deny responsibility for your accident, you are not surprised that my very strong suggestion is that you should consult with and then hire an experienced construction accident lawyer. There are too many things that can go wrong when handling a construction accident case. You want to hire someone who is a professional and who has years of experience dealing with these particular type of cases.

Remember, owners, contractors and their insurance companies will do everything in their power to minimize your claim, including blaming you for your own injuries, to avoid paying fair compensation for your damages. Don't help them by attempting to go it alone or by hiring a general practitioner without construction accident experience; give serious thought to hiring an experienced attorney to handle your construction accident claim, especially when the injuries are serious and permanent.

Many people do not know what an experienced construction accident lawyer can do in these types of cases. Here is a list of some of the types of services that we provide:

- Conduct initial interview with client.
- Educate client about the litigation process in a construction accident case.
- Notify all responsible parties and their insurance companies of our representation and that they are not permitted to speak with you. Demand that they preserve any evidence.
- Hire an investigator to gather evidence, interview witnesses, obtain accident reports, surveillance video and other relevant evidence.
- Retain construction accident experts as early as possible to inspect the accident scene or relevant dangerous equipment or conditions before repairs are made by the responsible party.
- Analyze legal issues relevant to your case, including possible defenses, such as recalcitrant worker defense or whether a municipal entity may be involved.

- Gather your medical records and other records that support your damages claims, including W-2s, employment records, and union and pension files.
- Commence the lawsuit by filing and serving a summons and complaint.
- Arrange for service of process of the summons and complaint on the defendants as required by law and file proof of service with the court.
- Serve responses to defendant's discovery demands.
- Communicate and meet with client's treating physicians to understand extent of injuries and prognosis.
- File a Request for Judicial Intervention (RJI) and request a court conference to order depositions and the exchange of further discovery.
- Communicate with the client regularly and client's treating physicians to keep up to date on your condition and better prepare your damages case.
- Hire expert economist to review your earnings record, union contracts, pension documents, social security record and work history as necessary to prepare a report on past and future economic losses.
- Hire expert physicians and/or other medical professionals, as necessary to establish causation and permanency of injuries as well as extent of any ongoing disability.

- Hire life-care planner and/or vocational rehabilitation expert to establish necessary future medical care and/or inability to perform gainful employment in the future.
- Review your workers' compensation lien to determine the amount paid for your medical care and wage loss to determine the amount to be repaid out of your case recovery.
- Prepare you for your deposition and appear with you at your deposition.
- Conduct the deposition of all defendants and other non-party witnesses that may have relevant information about your case.
- Prepare client and hire medical exam consultant to accompany client to the defendant's medical exams of client.
- Exchange expert disclosure to the defendant's attorney in support of client's claims.
- File a Note of Issue to advise the court that discovery is complete and the case is ready for trial.
- Research, draft, file and argue summary judgment motion on liability when necessary.
- Prepare client for trial testimony when necessary.
- Meet with and prepare expert witnesses for trial, including professional engineers, economists, vocational rehabilitation experts and physicians when necessary.

- Create and prepare trial exhibits.
- Organize records and other documentary evidence intended to be introduced at trial.
- Appear for court settlement conferences and mediation when necessary.
- Research and write trial briefs and argue trial motions.
- Select a jury and try the case before a judge over the course of a few days to a few weeks as necessary.
- Analyze jury verdict and judge's rulings to determine whether either side has any valid arguments for an appeal.
- Enter final judgment or prepare settlement papers and closing documents for payment by defendants.

This list is not exhaustive. But it will give you some idea of the type of work that may be necessary to successfully pursue a construction accident claim. This list is also intended to give you a framework of the timeline of your case.

Each case is different. Some cases may settle early, while others go all the way to trial. I have settled cases prior to filing the lawsuit and even settled cases after jury selection but before the verdict. There are always opportunities during the timeline of each case to discuss settlement with the opposing party. During the course of the case, we are in constant contact with our clients making sure they are informed at each stage as the case proceeds.

# CONCLUSION

NOW THAT YOU HAVE EDUCATED YOURSELF ON CONSTRUCTION accident cases in NYC and know the 7 biggest mistakes that can wreck your claim, you can better understand the legal process, know your rights when it comes to insurance companies and are equipped with being in a position to choose the best lawyer for your case. Congratulations.

You are ahead of the game by avoiding mistakes that can damage your construction accident case before it starts.

For more information, please visit our website at www.oconnorlawfirm.net. It has valuable resources, including helpful videos that you can use to further educate yourself and may answer additional questions you may have about your particular type of case. You can submit questions or call our office for further help.

Thank you for reading this book and good luck on making the right decisions in your own case.

*Brian J. O'Connor*

# CALL OUR OFFICE TODAY TO LEARN MORE

If you have been injured in a construction accident in New York City, call me today. Tell me your story. I will listen carefully and offer you some feedback. While we certainly can't guarantee any results, we may be the right law firm for you. If you feel comfortable with our talk, I will ask you to come in for a no fee, no obligation meeting. What happens after that could change your life. For the good. Call me at 212-566-4868 or 718-948-3500.

**Brian J. O'Connor** has been practicing law for more than 25 years and is passionate about helping injured New Yorkers get their lives back on track. Brian's commitment to excellence in personal injury has been recognized by his peers with numerous honors and awards over the years. Brian has been selected to the New York Metro Super Lawyers list, the National Trial Lawyers Top 100 Trial Lawyers, is *AV Preeminent* rated by Martindale-Hubbell, and has been featured in the *New York Law Journal's* Top Verdicts & Settlements. Brian is also a member of the Multi-Million Dollar Advocates Forum, the Irish Legal 100, the New York State Trial Lawyers Association and the American Association for Justice. The O'Connor Law Firm represents injured New Yorkers in the Bronx, Brooklyn, Manhattan, Queens and Staten Island in both State and Federal Courts.

WA

Made in the USA
Monee, IL
04 November 2026

67381829R10059